LIP MONSTERS

Momo Motormouth

Art by Victoria Greenwood   Words by Cynthia Baseman

To my nephew, Louie. As you grow, may your creativity and kindness grow with you.

V. G.

To my superstar brother, Greg, with love.

C. B.

Text copyright © 2023 by Cynthia Baseman

Illustrations copyright © 2023 by Victoria Greenwood

All rights reserved. For information about permission to reproduce selections from this book, email info@lipmonsters.com

Manufactured in the United States of America

Drifting clouds of squishy shapes

Reminded her of birthday cake.

Now which one would Mom bake?

Worm and jelly? Seaweed and vermicelli?

As long as it was super smelly.

Momo's brother Tom-Tom waved drumsticks. "Wait for me!"
"Not today, slow-poke, I have better places to be!"

Slugger and Hugger busted a move,
Tom-Tom tat-tatted a funky groove.

Sketch-scratch-scrape! Colors fly!
Back and forth went Pip's antenna eye.
Tinker's invention made a sizzling sound,
As always, Gar checked the Lost and Found.

"Thanks for reminding me about my teeth,
I'll brush and floss after each sugary sweet!"
Maddie translated and Willow whispered even more.
"Strong teeth and gums keep a mouth from being sore!"

No one seemed to remember. Momo turned away.
No one seemed to care that this was her birthday.

No hugs in homeroom or candy at lunch.
No parties with pickled cookies to crunch.

This is my day, not Willow's! Momo threw a fit.
I won't be ignored. Not for one little bit.
Eyeballs bulging, Momo went half-insane.
She clenched her fists as an idea hatched in her brain.

**No one wanted to hurt Momo's feelings on her special day.
Yet no one wanted to be mean to Willow. How could they?**

Willow slunk away, feeling so sad and hurt.
She buried her head in a pile of leaves and dirt.

Momo bragged about magic candles, wishes-come-true,
About birthday cakes colored pink, green and blue.

Teacher surprised them with pinecone pretzels and treesap tea.
Momo clapped and danced and sang, overcome with glee.
Tom-Tom drummed bong-bong-bong.
Monsters danced, getting along.

"It's all wrong! Bullying Willow is not a game!"
Momo knew Maddie was right. She was to blame.

Lip monsters went bumpity-bump-bumpity-bump.
Momo's crown fell to the floor with a giant thump.
She spun the silvery bolts upside-down.
Birthday smiles turned to birthday frowns.

Bad idea quickly changed his mind,
When Good idea said, "Please! Be kind!"

I promise to fix my mistake.
No matter how long that might take.

To the library they tip-toed first.
With no sign of Willow, Momo's heart almost burst.

They searched the community garden space.
The groundskeeper hadn't seen even a trace.

At the nurse's office, a monster lifted his head off a pillow.
No one there had caught a glimpse of Willow.

Tom-Tom slammed his favorite drum.
"Who will listen to my bum-bee-bum?"
Pip squeaked out loud and covered her ears.
"Who will jump rope with me?" she asked in tears.
Feeling lost and afraid, Hugger cried boo hoo hoo.
Slugger punched a hole in the wall, straight on through.
Gar checked Lost and Found. "It's no use," he yelped.
Tinker tried calling Moon on his space phone for help.

Willow whirled and twirled, wobbling to a standstill.
The monsters cheered, their voices loud and shrill.

"I'm sorry!" Momo cried, "I wanted everyone to love me."
Maddie translated: "We love you so, can't you see?"

Momo handed Willow the first piece of cake,
Willow thought hard about what wish to make.
Momo twisted her two bolts, smiling big as ever,
Then kissed her friend's cheek, light as a feather.
From one to the other, magic did flow,
Willow's sticky tentacles began to glow.
The crack in her heart healed as if by enchanted glue,
Being with her friends was the best gift of all, Momo knew.

The next day, Momo's big eyes opened wide.
One is for day! Two is for night! Three for X-raying inside.
When she spun silvery bolts on each side of her face,
All her worries disappeared without a trace.

Printed in the USA
CPSIA information can be obtained
at www.ICGtesting.com
LVHW061051121123
763674LV00025B/95